W9-BLR-128

HOW TO BECOME AN
AIRLINE PILOT

Achieve Your Dream
Without Going Broke

Robert Lawrence, ATP

Copyright © 2018
This book has been updated since its original publication in 2017.

Disclaimer: Every attempt has been made to provide up-to-date, accurate and reliable complete information. No warranties are implied. By reading this page the reader agrees that under no circumstances is the author responsible for any losses, direct or indirect, which are caused as a result of the use of the information contained within this book, including but not limited to – omissions, errors, and inaccuracies. Please note most of this publication is based on personal experience and secondary evidence. Use this information at your own expense, there is no guarantee for financial success.

HOW TO BECOME AN AIRLINE PILOT
Achieve Your Dream Without Going Broke
© ROBERT LAWRENCE / 2018.

No part of this book may be reproduced or transmitted in any form or by any means, mechanical or electronic. This includes photocopying, recording, or by any information storage and retrieval system. This book is for entertainment and educational purposes only and the views expressed are those of the author alone.

Contact Information

vegetarianpilot@gmail.com
howtobecomeanairlinepilot.org
robertlawrence.org

<u>Other great books by Robert Lawrence</u>

Happy Wife – Happy Life

A Survival Guide

A Day In The Life Of An Airline Pilot

A Much Better Life: Goal Setting, Visualization, & The Law
Of Attraction

TABLE OF CONTENTS

PREFACE

This book will benefit any aspiring pilot. Even if you only want to earn your private pilot's certificate, the helpful information in this book will save you time and lots of money.

I am currently an active pilot flying for one of the best airlines in the country. I became an airline pilot because several years ago I decided to pursue a career that would allow me to travel the world and experience a feeling of adventure at the same time.

While serving in the military in my late teens and early 20's I enjoyed parachuting from a variety of aircraft, so a career in aviation seemed like a good fit. However, I didn't know any pilots, I didn't have much money, and I was working full-time in a totally unrelated career. When I seriously considered becoming an airline pilot my inner doubts silently asked, "Who am I to believe I can become an airline pilot? I don't even know how to fly!" My inner doubts fought to keep me trapped inside my comfort zone. However, I beat back my doubts and fears by repeatedly telling myself, "If others can do it, I can do it too!"

Now that I'm actually living my dream, I understand that becoming an airline pilot was no different than pursuing any other goal. A journey of a thousand miles always begins with the first step. I took the first step and was confident that eventually I would arrive at my destination.

Your first step toward an airline career is reading this book. Once you take the first step you will be one step closer to your dream. Yes, you can become an airline pilot!

ACKNOWLEDGMENTS

I want to thank author and pilot Richard Bach. He inspired me to grow wings.

I would also like to thank Dave English of Great Aviation Quotes. Visit his website at: www.skygod.com

INTRODUCTION

"I was sold on flying as soon as I had a taste for it."

John Glenn

As I write this book there is a huge shortage of airline pilots. The shortage is so great that in 2015, at age 49, I was hired by an airline, despite having flown very little during the prior decade. Many of my classmates in airline ground school had spent a small fortune accumulating the required flight hours and pilot certificates, just for the opportunity to apply to a regional airline. However, I became an airline pilot without acquiring any debt. This book explains how you can achieve your dream of becoming an airline pilot without going broke; what you can anticipate during the journey, and what to expect after you are hired.

Most airlines still require (or strongly prefer) that you possess a four-year college degree. I suspect this requirement may be suspended as the pilot shortage worsens. But for now, a four-year college degree will definitely help you get hired. I was hired with an undergraduate degree in Political Science.

Regional airlines are the stepping stones which pave the way for you to be hired at a mainline carrier. The following regional airlines are currently operating in the United States: SkyWest, Mesa, Horizon, ExpressJet, Wisconsin Air, and numerous others. These airlines partner with larger domestic airlines, and some even allow their pilots to "flow through," to a mainline carrier. Flow through simply means that a regional pilot is guaranteed to get an interview with a partner airline, once he or she has acquired the minimum required flight experience.

Most of the airline pilots I have met began their airline careers by first flying for a regional airline, even if they only flew for the regional airline for three months before moving onto a larger carrier. The largest domestic airlines in the USA, such as Delta, American, United, and even Southwest, want to know that the pilots they hire are able to fly in an airline "crew environment" before investing tens of thousands of dollars training their new pilots. Remember, military pilots often fly solo during their military aviation careers, so flying in an airline crew environment might be new to them.

To be hired at a regional airline with no restrictions, you must possess a first class medical certificate; have accumulated 1,500 total flight hours; possess a multi-engine commercial pilot certificate, an instrument rating; and have successfully completed the written exam for the Airline Transport Pilot (ATP) certificate, with a passing score greater than 70%.

Currently, most, if not all regional airlines incur the cost of the practical (flight test) portion of your Airline Transport Certificate. Airlines now pay this expense because the competition for qualified pilots is steadily increasing. I suggest that you successfully complete the written ATP exam and **let the airline pay** for the flying portion of your ATP certificate. I just saved you thousands of dollars.

Of note, a quick internet search revealed that at least one regional airline is currently offering $60,000for first year pay. I suspect this amount includes a signing bonus and other incentives. However, what they're offering only proves that airlines are desperate to attract new pilots and they are aggressively competing for YOU! It is a great time to become an airline pilot.

WORDS OF ENCOURAGEMENT

The biggest obstacle to becoming an airline pilot is your belief in your ability to do so. If you have any doubt in your ability to achieve this, or any dream, read my book, *A BETTER LIFE, Goal Setting, Visualization, & The Law of Attraction*. If I can achieve my dream of becoming an airline pilot, YOU CAN TOO!

YES, YOU CAN BECOME AN AIRLINE PILOT

"I fly because it releases my mind from the tyranny of petty things..."

Antoine de Saint-Exupéry

To begin, the most important wisdom I can share is this, "Know with certainty that you can accomplish your goal of becoming an airline pilot." In life, people like to share their doubts and fears and tell others why something is too difficult or impossible to achieve. These people rarely achieve success in life and they never become pilots, let alone airline pilots. Right now, begin visualizing yourself as an airline pilot. Imagine yourself in your pilot uniform, sitting in the right seat of a commercial airliner. Imagine communicating with air traffic control (ATC), programming your flight computer and reading your checklist. Imagine taxiing to the runway, advancing the thrust levers, lifting off the runway at *Vr* (rotation speed) and climbing on course. Imagine you are engaging the autopilot, reaching cruising altitude, monitoring the aircraft systems, planning your arrival and approach, descending via the arrival procedure, flying the approach, and landing on the runway centerline with a smooth touchdown. Imagine taxiing to the gate, completing your before shutdown checklist, and saying goodbye to the passengers as they praise you for a great flight and a smooth landing.

Long before I became an airline pilot I imagined myself flying a commercial airliner. I followed the advice of Albert Einstein when he said, "Imagination is more important than knowledge..." A vivid imagination is vital, because like any challenge in life, obstacles will appear on your path. Don't let obstacles stop you from achieving your dream.

If you are not passionate about becoming an airline pilot you should not waste your time and money. Why? Because if you are not passionate about this, or any goal, every obstacle will seem insurmountable. However, the truth is that all obstacles can be overcome. If there were no obstacles in life we would rarely feel a sense of accomplishment. Try seeing obstacles as opportunities, and obstacles will become less daunting. People purchase jigsaw puzzles so they can solve a problem. Life is similar to assembling a puzzle. We must first visualize the outcome in our mind, and then take action. After taking several steps our path becomes clear, and in time, we arrive at our destination. This is how all problems in life are solved. The same is true for becoming an airline pilot. See flight training as a problem to be solved. The problem for you might be the expense, the time required to train, the complex subject matter, or the distance you live from a flight school. These obstacles are all problems that you can solve, just like a jigsaw puzzle. Don't focus on the problem; focus on the solution, because what you focus on will expand. The outcome will be you wearing your pilot uniform, flying a large jet aircraft. Problem solved.

Becoming an airline pilot will require discipline and commitment. If it was easy, everybody could become a pilot. However, most people simply do not believe they can accomplish such a lofty goal. Most people listen to their inner critic and defeat themselves mentally. That is why there are not many pilots in the world, let alone airline pilots. I suspect that at least 30% of student pilots who actually begin flight training never obtain their private pilot certificate, for one reason or another. I also suspect that most pilots, who do earn their private pilot certificate, never obtain or complete any additional flight training. That is fine. These are the same pilots who will help us acquire flight hours at little or no cost us (more about this later).

I want to emphasize that if you are dedicated and passionate about flying, you will become one of the few people whose office is located 35,000' above sea level. You will travel the world and eventually earn a six-figure annual income. Also, you will not have a boss breathing down your neck. It will just be you, your co-pilot, and a multi-million dollar aircraft. Sure, you will have passengers in your aircraft, but you will be secure behind the flight deck door. It is usually the flight attendants who have to interact with the occasional "difficult" passenger. Flying beats shuffling papers or digging trenches day after day. Believe me! I have worked numerous jobs during my life and nothing compares to being an airline pilot.

FINDING THE RIGHT FLIGHT SCHOOL

"I might have been born in a hovel, but I determined to travel with the wind and the stars."

Jackie Cochran

Most people begin flight training by simply driving to the nearest airport flight school and telling the person behind the counter that they want to learn to fly. This is the most convenient method to begin your flight training. However, it may not be the most effective way to begin pilot training. Almost every airport has one or more flight schools on site. Each school offers lessons and introductory flights. Take an introductory flight before you embark on your journey. If you get in the plane and find that you're absolutely terrified, maybe an airline career is not for you. Don't spend more than $100 on an introductory flight. The school will usually accept a financial loss because they hope the introductory flight will convince you to sign up for lessons at their school. Before you drive to the airport, search online for an introductory flight "offer," as prices vary considerably.

You should understand that every flight school exists for the sole purpose of earning income for the flight school owner(s). A flight school is a for-profit business. The owner(s) of the flight school will try to sell you more than just flight training. They will try to sell you an expensive aviation headset, several study guides, paper and digital charts, gadgets of every kind, flight simulator training sessions, shirts, pilot jackets, emblems, sunglasses, and anything which may be profitable to them. I will explain what you have to purchase in my next chapter so you do not overspend on items you do not need, can borrow, or find elsewhere for less money.

I began my first flying job working at a local flight school and here is what I learned: Most instructors are working at flight schools in order to accrue sufficient flight hours so they can eventually obtain employment with an airline, or maybe land a corporate flying job. The danger is this: when you begin training at your local flight school you might be assigned to fly with an instructor who has already accumulated 1,400 flight hours. Then, one day you show up for a lesson and your instructor is no longer employed there, because he, or she, was hired by Acme Airlines. If, and when, this happens, you will have to begin training with a different flight instructor who is also hoping to be hired elsewhere. This turnover can cause you to spend extra money because you might have to repeat training in order to convince the "new" instructor that you're capable of advancing to the next lesson. Sadly, this is the nature of flight instructing, for the most part.

Flight instructing is usually low paying and stressful work, and most instructors are not interested in flight instructing as a career. Rather, flight instructing is generally viewed as a stepping stone to an airline career. I must note that many pilots choose to make flight instructing their profession and I am grateful for them!

You must keep in mind that you can select your instructor. It is your right because you are the paying customer. Ask the flight school manager about the credentials of each instructor. Ask how long each instructor has worked at the flight school. Interview your instructor before you fly with him or her. Flight training is a customer service business and you are the customer. If the instructor is rude or does not communicate effectively, find another instructor. If your instructor has a disheveled appearance, move on. Your instructor should inspire confidence. After all, you will be sharing a tiny space with this person and their job is to keep you safe and teach you how to fly. If you don't have a good rapport with your instructor, it will not be an enjoyable experience. I have had many great instructors. Insist on the best. Don't be afraid to fire your flight instructor if you're not happy. You are the customer and you must do what is best for you.

A great flight instructor respects your time, has amazing patience, and communicates effectively. A great flight instructor tells you what subject matter to study before you arrive for your lesson, reviews each lesson with you before you fly, ensures you understand what is expected during the lesson, and has unending patience.

Flight instructors are generally paid in 6-minute increments. For example, each six minute block is billed as .1 flight hour, or ground instruction. If I was your flight instructor, and we flew together for 1 hour, 18 minutes, I would bill you for 1.3 hours of instruction. I would also bill you accordingly for any ground instruction I provided. You will also have to pay for all the time the aircraft engine is operating.

The cost of the airplane is billed similarly to flight instruction. The rental plane has a "meter" installed, much like a taxi cab. If you fly the airplane for 1 hour, 30 minutes, you will be billed for 1.5 hours of aircraft rental. Currently, the rental expense for a Cessna Skyhawk, or a similar general aviation aircraft, varies from $125 to $175 hourly, more or less. The aircraft is generally rented 'wet.' The term wet simply means that the cost of fuel is included in the rental charge. If the fuel is not included in the rental price, you should be aware that aviation fuel varies widely in price, depending on the airport and fuel provider. If you are paying for your own fuel, there are aviation "apps" available, so that you can locate the cheapest aviation fuel. Currently, aviation fuel costs more than $4 per gallon at my local airport. A small, general aviation aircraft might burn 8-12 gallons of aviation fuel per hour. With a simple calculation you can understand that paying for flight instruction and aircraft rental can be an expensive endeavor. Nonetheless, you can learn to fly and accumulate 1,500 flight hours without going broke.

Flight Instructors will usually schedule lessons for two hours or longer. Let's say your lesson is scheduled from noon until 2 p.m. If you are scheduled to fly on a particular day, you should arrive at the airport early and pre-flight the aircraft. You don't need to pay for your instructor to watch you perform your preflight inspection before every lesson. Arrive 15 minutes early and ensure the airplane is fueled and airworthy, then go inside and be prepared to meet with your instructor for your pre-flight briefing.

Your instructor should be on time. Delays happen in aviation, I understand that. However, your time is valuable. If your instructor is habitually tardy, fire him or her. Don't feel bad. You are the customer and you are spending too much money to put up with bad service. Flight training is a service oriented business and you probably have lots of options available to you.

Before each flight, your instructor should conduct a lesson review and answer questions about the material you have studied, and he or she should also review what you can expect during your lesson. The airplane is noisy, even while wearing aviation headsets, so make sure you understand what is expected before you fly.

In the classroom, your instructor will have the use of images and diagrams to illustrate a particular flight maneuver. Before you get into the airplane, ensure you fully understand what is expected in slow flight, or during a stall recovery, etc. Learning about and then performing a flight maneuver for the first time when you are in a noisy airplane is an ineffective teaching strategy and suggests that your instructor is not looking out for your best interests.

During the lesson your instructor must be dedicated to you, and only you. If they are distracted with lunch, or he or she is "texting" during your lesson, make a note. If you arrive at the plane and find yourself waiting several minutes for your instructor to arrive, make a note. If your instructor is not prepared for your lesson, make a note. Tally up the wasted time and insist that the time be deducted from your bill. At the end of each lesson, check with the flight desk and see what the instructor has billed for that lesson. If your numbers do not agree, find out why. If anyone tries to make you feel guilty, talk to the flight school manager to resolve the issue, or seek training elsewhere. If your instructor is adding .2 or .3 billable hours on every training session, at the end of twenty lessons you could be overpaying by hundreds of dollars, or much more. Do not tolerate this. I must say that very few instructors behave this way. However, I have seen it happen, so I suggest you follow my advice so you do not overpay. I want you to become an airline pilot without going broke. I must point out that MOST instructors actually "under the bill" their students. Your flight instructor is a highly trained, competent pilot, and he or she probably invested thousands of hours studying and training before they earned the privilege of becoming a certified flight instructor. They are professionals!

Instead of "paying as you go" for flight instruction at your local flight school, a more efficient way to obtain flight instruction may be to purchase a "package deal" from a flight school. A package deal will include a "fixed-price" for both the instructor and aircraft rental. For example, a flight school may offer to provide the required flight training in a fixed number of days, so that you can obtain your private pilot certificate for $9,000, for example. If you instead choose to participate in weekly training at your local flight school, you might expect to pay $12,000 for the same training, as it will likely take more flight hours to earn your certificate. The cost estimates listed above are just that, estimates. The cost of training varies greatly across the country, so do your due diligence in order to get the best deal. In my opinion, the best way to learn to how to fly is to fly as often as you can. It's like practicing piano. The more often you practice, the better you become and the quicker you become proficient.

You can search online for package deals at various flight schools across the country. When a school offers a package deal, the school has an interest in teaching you efficiently and cost effectively, because the quicker you earn your certificate or rating, the more profit the flight school can earn. The instructors at these flight schools are usually paid a salary, so they have no incentive to "drag out" your training. This type of flight training often requires you to travel some distance from your home but the cost savings might make this the best option.

After overpaying at a variety of local flight schools I eventually obtained my commercial pilot certificate and flight instructor ratings at a fixed-cost flight school, located several hours from my home. I obtained instruction at a great discount because I had reviewed the appropriate study guides at home, and arrived at the flight school ready to fly, and prepared to take the written exam. You will usually need an instructor with you in the airplane during flight training, but most of the "ground school" learning you can acquire alone, without having to pay an instructor to look over your shoulder. When you are studying at home, remember to highlight questions which may require additional explanation, and then ask your instructor about those specific questions during your next lesson.

I will not recommend a particular flight school in this book as flight school management changes over time, and a great school one year may not be a great school the following year. However, you can complete your research online and determine what's best for you. Instead of just viewing a particular flight school's website, take the time to read recent customer reviews to learn what other pilots have to say about their experience there. Several negative customer reviews might persuade me to look elsewhere.

Some aviation enthusiasts are opposed to training in fixed-price flight schools, arguing that you're not getting the best training when a school is trying to cram a month of flight training into one week. However, you will only earn your pilot certificate, or rating, when the FAA examiner is convinced that you meet or exceed the FAA standards. I understand the concerns that aviation enthusiasts might have, given that your initial flight training is the foundation from which all subsequent training will be based. However, every airline will train their new hire pilots to fly to their specific standards before they allow you to sit in the flight deck of one of their multi-million dollar aircraft. Furthermore, by flying with a variety of pilots and instructors over the course of your training, you will be exposed to both good and "not so good" pilots, so you can learn what to do correctly, and what not to do in an airplane. There is no substitute for experience. I believe I became a better pilot by flying with a variety of pilots and instructors.

Some young pilot candidates prefer to combine their college education with flight training. I know several pilots who have done this. A few public universities are known for their flight training programs, and some private colleges also offer great flight training. I am not opposed to this route, if you are not in a hurry, have not yet earned a college degree, and you have plenty of money to spend. Do what is right for you. I will tell you this; some of the best pilots I have flown with are simply the most passionate about flying. They learned to fly at their local flight school and their lives revolve around aviation. When you are passionate about aviation it really does not matter where you obtained your flight training. What is important is what you do with the time you are in flight school. Were you studying? Were you interested in the subject matter? Were you passionate? If the answer to any of the questions is, "no," then it doesn't matter where you learned to fly. Regardless, I suggest that you remain focused on your goal of becoming an airline pilot. Obtain your training as quickly and as affordably as possible and get hired by an airline. Once you're flying for a profession you will become a better pilot, regardless of where you obtained your initial training.

Airline flying is very different than flying in a Cessna Skyhawk or Piper Warrior on the weekend. Airline pilots have the assistance of dispatchers who create flight plans, and onboard flight computers, which load flight plans and calculate fuel burn and much more. When you apply to become an airline pilot it is understood that you already know how to fly; the real question will become, "Can you learn to manage aviation technology and work in a crew environment?" Trust me, airlines do not care if you can fly a perfect lazy 8 pattern. Flying a lazy 8 pattern is a skill you need to demonstrate in order to earn your commercial pilot license. Once you demonstrate proficiency flying a lazy 8 pattern, you will probably never again fly a lazy 8 pattern. It's like much of the information you learned in high school or college. In college, I had to master calculus in order to graduate. I have long since forgotten how to perform calculus, but it was a hurdle I had to overcome in order to advance in my college career. Flight training is similar. Learn what is required, and then move on to the next phase of training.

HOW TO PAY FOR FLIGHT TRAINING

"The very existence of aviation is proof that man, given the will, has the capacity to accomplish deeds that seem impossible."

Eddie Rickenbacker

I worked three jobs to pay for my flight training. Instead of borrowing, I only spent money on flight training that I had already earned. It took me a little longer to complete my required training but I became an airline pilot without accruing any debt.

I have met several pilots who found jobs working at the local airport when they began their flight training, because they believed that being around airplanes and mingling with other pilots gave them an advantage. However, airport-related jobs generally don't pay much, so I chose to work elsewhere for higher wages, so I could pay for more flight training. I worked for the government during the week and on weekends and nights I worked as a wedding DJ and occasionally as a "blackjack" dealer at corporate parties. My "side jobs" earned me tips, in addition to a great part-time income. I was able to fly three times weekly. I don't know where I found the time to fly and study, but I did, because I was passionate and determined to become a pilot. I also rented the cheapest planes available because flight time acquired in a Cessna 150 counts the same as flight time accrued in a Skylane.

If you intend to borrow money to pay for flight training, the interest on the loan usually begins accruing immediately. Therefore, it is important to borrow money at the lowest possible interest rate and begin repaying the debt as soon as you're able. Borrow money only if you're in a hurry to become an airline pilot. Your first job at a regional airline might only pay $40,000 (or less) the first year, and you may have additional expenses such as paying rent at a "crash pad," if your domicile is located far from your home (more on this later). It takes time to begin earning the big dollars as an airline pilot, so please be careful if you choose to borrow money to pay for training. Several of my classmates in ground school had borrowed over $125,000 to pay for flight training and they hadn't made a single payment toward their debt when I had met them. That's like paying a home mortgage but not having a home. Ouch!

Please don't cash out your retirement savings to pay for flight training. You will regret this later in life. I would suggest paring down your expenses by driving a used car, finding a roommate, buying used flight training equipment, and giving up expensive coffees, pay television channels, and eliminating another non-essential spending. You will be too busy studying for the next year to do much else anyway. Save money now so you will not be paying thousands of dollars in interest later. You will thank me in five years if you take this advice.

A final note on this topic: Flight training scholarships may be available for some pilot candidates. A search of "aviation scholarships" online returned a variety of websites advertising aviation scholarships. Also, female pilot applicants might find additional financial grants available at www.ninety-nines.org.

WHAT YOU NEED TO PURCHASE

"I have often said that the lure of flying is the lure of beauty. That the reasons flyers fly, whether they know it or not, is the aesthetic appeal of flying."

Amelia Earhart

As I mentioned earlier, flight schools will try to sell you everything and anything. Every flight school has display cases full of shiny gadgets and trinkets. The flight school employees might suggest that you need to purchase a variety of their merchandise to make learning to fly easier. Save your money. You don't need to purchase a fuel strainer. You also don't need to purchase an expensive flight bag. The flight school should provide most of what you need and you can borrow study guides or purchase lightly used study guides on eBay or Amazon. Always check to see what training material is available online before purchasing paper documents or books. Here are the basic items that you need to purchase when you are learning to fly:

1. Aviation headset
2. Aviation charts
3. Plotter&E6B flight computer (whiz wheel)
4. Pilot logbook
5. Medical certificate

Aviation headset

A small airplane with its engine and propeller located just a few feet in front of the cockpit makes for a very loud environment. It is stressful and uncomfortable to be subjected to loud noises, hour after hour. Therefore, do not be a cheapskate when purchasing your headset. Pay a little more to protect your hearing and make your flying experience more enjoyable.

I have two suggestions when deciding which headset is best for you. First, I suggest you consider purchasing a lightly used headset online. You can find used headsets for a fraction of the cost of a new headset. Fortunately for you, lots of aspiring pilots purchased new, expensive aviation headsets before they took their first flight lesson. Soon thereafter, they may have surrendered their dream of becoming a pilot, for whatever reason, and now they are selling their headset online. Sometimes the aspiring pilot had to quit because a new baby was on the way, or they realized that learning to fly was more difficult than they had imagined, or they found they had no passion for flying. Regardless, their loss can be your gain. I suggest that any headset you purchase be a "noise canceling."

In the past, I have purchased headsets that weighed too much, squeezed my head and lacked noise canceling technology. Looking back, I should not have endured the suffering as long as I did, but I didn't know any better. Inexpensive and uncomfortable headsets are tolerable on flights lasting an hour or less, but will become a distraction on longer flights, and they're not suited for the long distance flights you'll be conducting as an airline pilot. Therefore, I suggest you budget $500 and purchase a lightweight, comfortable, lightly used noise canceling headset online. The headset you purchase for $500 may have sold new for $1,000 only weeks earlier.

I personally use a Bose QC15 noise canceling headset (since discontinued), which I purchased new at costco.com. I then purchased a separate microphone online from UFlyMike.com. It was the best money I ever spent. If the Bose headset is no longer available when you're reading this book, purchase a lightly used, noise canceling aviation headset online. Read customer reviews to ensure you get the best headset for the money. Lots of airline pilots prefer Bose headsets.

Aviation Charts

Every pilot must have access to aviation charts. When you begin flight training you will only need visual flight rule (VFR) sectional charts. When you are training for your instrument rating you will need instrument flight rules (IFR) charts. Currently, aviation charts are available in both paper and digital form. Also, the FAA website allows users to download aviation charts. Your instructor will let you know what charts you need.

I used paper charts for years and several times annually a new sectional chart was issued, so I continually had to purchase charts. It was a never ending expense. Also, paper charts are cumbersome and hard to read when flying, especially at night. My current employer uses Jeppesen digital charts. My airline also issues all its pilots a tablet computer which is loaded with all our required charts and company manuals etc. I bet you already own an iPad or some other tablet. If so, purchase Jeppesen digital aviation charts. You will be expected to decipher Jeppesen charts when you're hired by an airline, so I suggest you skip the government charts and purchase a digital subscription from Jeppesen and upload the charts to your tablet. The digital charts will have to be updated occasionally, but it's accomplished with only an Internet connection. Digital charts also make flight planning much easier. Again, ask your flight instructor before you purchase any charts.

Plotter & E6B flight computer (whiz wheel)

When you initially begin flight training you will be expected to use a plotter and E6B flight computer. An E6B flight computer isn't a modern day computer. It's a rigid paper slide rule with a wheel attached. Don't let the name intimidate you. With modern technology the need for a plotter and an E6B flight computer is unnecessary, in my opinion, but the FAA is slow to change. Not every pilot has access to, or uses digital charts and computerized flight planning, so I suspect you will still be expected to demonstrate proficiency with these tools. Both can be purchased online for less than $20. The plotter and flight computer are used to compute wind correction angles and magnetic deviation, etc. I have long ago forgotten how to use either tool. Fortunately, you won't be expected to know how to use either tool when you're hired as an airline pilot. Ask your instructor if you will be required to demonstrate proficiency using the mechanical E6B flight computer and plotter during training. If not, simply download an E6B "app" to your tablet and/or mobile phone and use the technology to your advantage.

Pilot Logbook

When I began flight training I purchased the least expensive (paper) pilot logbook available. I still use it. However, I suggest that you make your life easier and also purchase an inexpensive electronic logbook. Electronic logbooks are available from a variety of providers. The most important function, in my opinion, is the ability to sync your logbook via a variety of platforms. Meaning, you can enter flight time on your mobile phone, and the data is automatically synced to your tablet and/or laptop computer. There is endless research available online regarding electronic logbooks. However, when you begin training, I suggest you simply ask a couple of flight instructors what electronic logbook they're using, and then make an informed decision. When you've purchased your electronic logbook, after each flight just enter the data into the app on your mobile phone or tablet and your life will be much easier when it is time to apply to an airline.

Medical Certificate

I suggest that during your first flight physical exam you request a 1st class medical certificate. I make this suggestion because an airline will require you to possess a 1st class medical certificate when you are hired. During your initial training you will only need to possess a third-class medical certificate. However, make sure you qualify for a 1st class medical certificate when you begin training, so you don't accumulate 1,500 flight hours and then discover that poor health is preventing you from becoming an airline pilot.

Prices for medical certificates vary considerably, so shop around. I currently pay $125 to obtain a 1st class medical certificate. However, in the past I have paid over $300 for the same certificate because I failed to compare prices. The flight physical can last anywhere from 10 minutes to an hour. Although it's an exam, there is no need to study!

HOW TO ACQUIRE FLIGHT HOURS
WITHOUT PAYING

"The Wright Brothers created the single greatest cultural force since the invention of writing. The airplane became the first World Wide Web, bringing people, languages, ideas, and values together."

Bill Gates

During my life, I have learned that both working class and wealthy people purchase sailboats and airplanes. These same people usually enjoy the company of others when sailing or flying. Early on in my piloting career, a mentor told me, "Remember OPP." I asked what OPP meant and my mentor replied, "Other peoples' planes." It was great advice. Both boats and airplanes are money pits. Never purchase a boat or an airplane! Just make friends with people who own airplanes and/or boats. This has always been my strategy and I have had access to airplanes and boats for the past 20 years.

Once you learn to fly you can advertise yourself on the community message board at local airports and on the Craigslist website. Post an advertisement which indicates that you are available to fly, and note what licenses and ratings you possess. A fellow pilot with a plane, or access to a plane, will eventually reach out and ask if you want to fly together. Most pilots only fly occasionally and they probably have doubts about their abilities, or they just want some company while they are flying. These pilots are great assets. Often, they are wealthy professionals who bought an airplane after earning their private pilot license. Now, they have an airplane and they don't fly as often as they like and feel more comfortable having another licensed pilot seated next to them. I have always felt that flying is a team sport. One pilot should always be flying the aircraft and be on the lookout for other aircraft, especially when the other pilot is reviewing aviation charts, etc.

Airlines utilize crew resource management (CRM) on every flight. Therefore, you should get used to flying as either the pilot flying (PF) or the pilot monitoring (PM). It is proven to be safer when pilots divide flying duties and it will make for an easier transition to airline flying if you begin utilizing these roles early in your pilot training.

By advertising myself on websites and local message boards I accumulated hundreds of flight hours at little or no cost to me. The person with the airplane felt better having another pilot onboard and I felt better knowing that I was accruing free flight time. Often, I paid a portion of the fuel expense. Other times, it wasn't expected. You can enter the flight time into your pilot logbook, provided that you are actually flying the plane. This strategy is much less expensive than renting a plane from a flying club or a fixed base operator (FBO) at your local airport.

After earning my commercial pilot certificate and Certified Flight Instructor (CFI) ratings, I found that lots of pilots asked me to fly with them. My job was to keep them safe. In exchange, I flew at least 50% of the time and logged the flight time in my logbook as pilot in command (PIC). The other pilot got the benefit of my experience and my company, and I got the benefit of their company and the use of their airplane! This tip alone can save you tens of thousands of dollars.

If you choose to earn your Certified Flight Instructor (CFI) rating you can log all the time you fly with another pilot, provided you are actually providing instruction. You can work for a flight school or you can work for yourself. I caution that if you work for yourself as a CFI, ensure you purchase adequate insurance to protect yourself and your assets, should one of your students ever become involved in an accident. If your signature appears in another pilot's logbook, and that pilot has a mishap later on, an attorney may come after you for negligence. I am not saying it is fair, but just know that a flight instructor rating comes with lots of responsibility. Protect your pilot certificate and your financial assets by purchasing appropriate insurance, when appropriate.

If you choose to fly with a pilot who owns his or her own plane, or who is renting a plane, please ensure the maintenance on the plane is current. You will also want to become comfortable flying the particular make and model plane in the traffic pattern before you embark on a cross-country journey, or before flying at night or in the clouds. When you fly a variety of planes you will soon learn that the throttle, gauges, flap controls, etc. are always located in a different location than the last plane you flew. It takes time to learn the various switch positions, and in an emergency you don't want to find yourself searching for the fuel selector or some other knob.

When discussing flying, I always stress safety over all else. If you're not comfortable about the weather, aircraft maintenance or your abilities; don't fly. It is always better to be safe than sorry in aviation. As a flight instructor, I encountered a good pilot who later died because he made a bad decision in an airplane. I also encountered a few pilots who never should have been granted their certificates because they lacked good judgment. However, I have mostly encountered lots of great pilots. They all look normal on the ground, but you never know their skill level until you're sitting next to him or her in the airplane, several thousand feet in the sky. I have seen pilots "freeze up" when an unexpected situation exceeded their piloting skills, so do not rely on another pilot to save you from a bad situation.

REQUIRED FLIGHT CERTIFICATES AND RATINGS

"There isn't a flight that goes by when I don't stare out of the window and thank my stars for what I'm seeing and feeling."

Richard Branson

To begin this section of the book I will outline what flight certificates and ratings you need to obtain employment as an airline pilot.

Private pilot certificate

The first license you will need to earn is your private pilot certificate. The requirements can be found in FAR 61.102. To qualify for your private pilot certificate you will need to meet the following criteria:

1. Be at least 17 years of age.

2. Be able to read, write, and converse fluently in English.

3. Obtain at least a third-class FAA medical certificate.

4. Receive and log ground training from an authorized instructor or complete a home-study course.

5. Pass a knowledge test with a score of 70% or better. The private pilot knowledge test consists of 60 multiple-choice questions selected from all of the airplane-related questions in the FAA's private pilot knowledge test bank.

6. Accumulate appropriate flight experience (see FAR 61.109). Receive a total of 40 hours of flight instruction and solo flight time.

7. Receive flight instruction and demonstrate the skill (see FAR 61.107).

8. Successfully complete a practical (flight) test, which will be given as a final exam by an FAA inspector or designated pilot examiner; it will be conducted as specified in the FAA's Private Pilot Practical Test Standards.

The above requirements appear to be overwhelming at first glance. However, trust that each requirement will build upon prior knowledge.

The first official written test you must prepare for is the private pilot exam. Before you are able to take the exam, you must obtain your flight instructor's signature in your logbook. The requirements for the private pilot exam are outlined in FAR 61.35.

The federal aviation rules and regulations can be found in book form, or online in a digital format. The regulations are written by attorneys so they can be confusing to non-lawyers. You can search for specific aviation regulations online by entering faa.gov into your computer browser. At faa.gov you will find the Federal Aviation Administration website with all their directives, regulations, and guidelines. To begin your search, I suggest you look under Licenses & Certificates, Regulations & Policies, and Training & Testing. There is too much information to memorize, obviously. Therefore, the important thing is that you learn where to "locate" certain information.

Here is a tip I learned too late in my training: During your initial training you will mostly be required to learn about flight regulations located in FAR Parts 61 and 91. A general rule of thumb is to search for pilot requirements in Part 61, and airplane requirements in Part 91. This statement is an oversimplification. However, keep this in mind and you might save valuable time when you're searching for a regulation during an oral examination.

As I mentioned above, FAR Part 61 relates to the certification of pilots. FAR Part 61 discusses, for example; medical certificates, alcohol use, name changes, and knowledge test requirement. All these topics are related to the requirements of pilots, as opposed to the aircraft we fly. For example, if you are asked a question during an oral exam regarding the flight experience required for a pilot to take off and land with passengers, after sunset, you should know where to locate the information. Since the question asks information related to the requirements of the "pilot," you would search for the answer in FAR 61. In fact, the answer can be found in FAR 61.57(3)(b).

FAR Part 91 discusses general operating and flight rules. For example, aircraft speeds, altitudes, airspace, and fuel requirements are topics discussed in FAR Part 91. These requirements deal more with the aircraft and the environment than they do with pilots.

Don't worry too much. When you begin studying for your written and oral exams you will use study guides to learn answers to the questions you will be expected to know. You will discover that there is information you will have to memorize, and other information you will only need to know where it can be found. Set aside several hours weekly to study and you will be fine.

Pilot study guides are sold by Jeppesen, Sporty's, Gleim, and numerous other companies. Personally, I studied for all of my flight exams using Gleim books. I cannot say if Gleim study books are superior to other study guides. However, I easily passed all my written exams using Gleim books. I still have them. You can purchase new or used study guides on the internet. New study guides are also sold at nearly every flight school. However, to save money I suggest you purchase lightly used study guides online. The information within the study guides rarely changes and once you're done with a study guide you might never reference it again. That is why I suggest you save your money and buy lightly used study guides or ask your instructor or another pilot if you can borrow their guides. Most pilots have a stack of study guides stashed away somewhere and they will probably be happy to let you borrow them. All pilots know it can be challenging to pay for flight training, so we are usually happy to help our fellow pilots.

Instrument rating

After you earn your private pilot license you should begin training to obtain your instrument rating. The addition of an instrument rating to your pilot certificate will make you a better pilot. It will also allow you to fly on days when a cloud layer is obscuring the horizon and most other pilots are grounded. Where I live in coastal California, for several months each year a cloud layer blankets the coast. The cloud layer is often only 500' thick, but the layer is thick enough to keep most pilots grounded. With an instrument rating a pilot can file an instrument flight plan (or request VFR on top) and depart the airport, climb through the clouds, and emerge above the clouds in less than one minute. Above the clouds the sun is shining and the surrounding mountains appear as islands in the sky. The skies are not crowded on these days because only pilots with instrument ratings are flying. Without an instrument rating your training might be delayed, so obtain your instrument rating as soon as practical.

Currently, to earn an instrument rating a pilot must first obtain his or her private pilot certificate, and then acquire at least 50 total hours of cross-country flight time; at least 40 hours of actual or simulated instrument flight time; and at least 15 hours of instrument flight training from an authorized instructor. Consult FAR 61.65 for all the requirements of the instrument rating.

The flight school where you obtain your instrument flight training might pressure you to purchase "foggles." Foggles resemble large, ugly sunglasses, and are intended to restrict your outside vision and eliminate your ability to see the horizon, as if you are flying in the clouds or in poor visibility. I suggest that you do not purchase any view limiting devices, to include foggles. The flight school should provide you with a view limiting device during training, so do not spend money on equipment that the flight school already possesses.

Earning your instrument rating requires you to interpret and trust your flight instruments and ignore your "gut feeling." When you cannot see the horizon your inner ear tells your brain that you're climbing or turning left, when you're actually descending and turning right. Our "sense" of up, down, right, and left becomes confused. Much of your instrument flight training involves overcoming your instincts and learning to trust your aircraft instruments.

While pursuing your instrument rating you will also learn how to read instrument charts, learn how to file instruments flight plans, and how to comply with instrument flight rules (IFR).

As an airline pilot all your flying will comply with instrument flight rules. Meaning, you will fly at different altitudes than aircraft which are not flying on an IFR flight plan. Most weekend pilots do not file flight plans and they fly at altitudes ending in 500'. For example, 3,500' or 6,500' or 9,500' etc., depending on the direction of travel. When flying in the clouds, on an instrument flight plan, pilots must fly at altitudes ending in 1,000'. For example, 7,000' or 20,000' or 37,000' etc., depending upon the direction of travel. This is how we separate aircraft flying in different directions and on different flight plans. You will learn more about these regulations during your training. Just know that there is a reason for the various altitudes.

Another note of caution here: Always choose to stay on the ground or land if you have any doubts about your flying abilities, the weather, or the aircraft. Prior to becoming an airline pilot I chose not to fly, rented a car, and drove home on more than one occasion. I did this because external conditions exceeded my abilities, or confidence, or the general aviation aircraft I was flying had no ice protection. Minimum weather and pilot requirements exist for our safety, for the safety of our passengers, and the safety of those on the ground. Follow the rules established by the FAA and you will be fine.

Commercial certificate

After you have obtained your instrument rating, the next pilot certificate you should earn is your commercial certificate (FAR 61.121). I obtained both single engine and multi-engine commercial pilot certificates. If you expect to earn money flying single engine aircraft you will need the single-engine commercial pilot certificate. I obtained both single and multi-engine commercial certificates because I planned on becoming a flight instructor, en-route to becoming an airline pilot, and most flight instruction is performed in single engine aircraft. However, if you're not interested in earning income flying single engine aircraft, just acquire your multi-engine commercial pilot certificate.

The commercial pilot certificate is challenging to obtain because it bestows upon you the privileges of a professional pilot; meaning, you can earn income as a pilot. To earn your commercial certificate you will have to demonstrate proficiency by flying advanced maneuvers. The commercial pilot certificate will also require you to obtain a high level of familiarity and understanding of numerous FAA regulations. However, once you reach this point in your training nothing is going to stop you.

Multi-engine rating

The multi-engine rating allows you to pilot an aircraft with more than one engine. There are no minimum flight time requirements to obtain your multi-engine rating. However, you will need to obtain an endorsement from your flight instructor before taking the practical test. As always, the test is administered by an FAA examiner or a designated pilot examiner. The practical test will never be administered by your flight instructor. There is no written exam required for the multi-engine rating. However, the FAA examiner will require you to pass an oral exam. The oral exam is usually conducted prior to the practical flight test.

On average, you can expect to receive approximately 10 hours of flight instruction in a multi-engine aircraft before you are prepared to take the practical test. Most of the training involves the instructor simulating that one engine is inoperative. Meaning, your instructor will reduce thrust on one engine, to simulate the loss of power in that engine. The loss of power in one engine changes the performance and aerodynamics of the aircraft. Among other requirements, pilots must compensate for the loss of thrust and maintain directional control of the aircraft to pass their practical exam.

During your multi-engine training, I suggest renting the cheapest twin-engine airplane available, provided it is mechanically sound. You don't need to rent an expensive twin-engine plane that is loaded with the latest avionics and other additional equipment during your multi-engine training. You will have your hands full just trying to keep the airplane flying straight and level. Also, the training will generally be conducted in good visibility weather. I rented an older Beechcraft Duchess during my multi-engine training and the Duchess got the job done just fine. What I am getting at is this; there is no need to pay for a "glass cockpit," unless you're going to be using the technology. When able, always conduct training in a less expensive airplane. A glass cockpit means that the gauges are displayed on a screen, much like your computer monitor, as opposed to the flight instruments found in older airplanes. Instruments often found in older aircraft are commonly referred to as "steam gauges." You will likely encounter both old and new avionics during your training. Just be sure to use the equipment if you're paying for it. You won't need a glass cockpit during your multi-engine flight training. However, if there is no price difference when renting the plane, always choose a plane with a glass cockpit, as "glass displays" are becoming more commonplace and that's generally what you'll encounter as an airline pilot, in most cases.

You can rent airplanes for a lower hourly rate if you purchase "block time." Meaning, you pay for a block of 10 or more rental hours. It's like renting a car. If you rent a car for one week you can expect to pay a lower daily rate than if you rent a car for only one day.

Currently, some regional airlines only require applicants to have 25 total hours of multi-engine flight time to be hired. I was hired by an airline with only 75 hours of multi-engine flight time. Multi-engine flight time is expensive to purchase, so only purchase the minimum flight time required by the regional airline where you want to work.

Flight instructor (not required)

The most common strategy to accrue flight hours is to become a flight instructor. A flight instructor rating is not required to become an airline pilot, but most pilots in my airline class had been working as flight instructors prior to being hired. My class also included three pilots who had served in the military, prior to becoming airline pilots.

After earning my commercial pilot certificate I immediately began training to obtain my flight instructor rating (FAR 61.181).I obtained my flight instructor rating by studying for the written exam at home. In subject areas where I lacked comprehension, I asked my instructor to clarify the subject matter. When my instructor and I agreed that I was ready to take the written exam I made an appointment to take the test at an authorized testing facility, located at a local flight school. Upon completion of the test I obtained a certificate which indicated I had passed the written exam.

Next, I compared prices and customer reviews at a variety of flight schools which offered a fixed-price flight instructor rating. When I found a suitable school, I used vacation time to escape work and traveled to the out-of-state flight school. At the fixed-price flight school I flew early in the morning and late into the evening. When the instructor was satisfied with my performance, he approved me to take the practical test with an FAA examiner. I passed the exam and was then authorized to begin teaching other pilots to fly.

Taking a practical flight test with an FAA examiner can be stressful. However, just fly as you have been trained and you should be fine. After all, your flight instructor will not "recommend" you for the practical test until he or she is confident you will pass the exam.

After I had obtained my certified flight instructor rating I next trained for and earned my certified flight instructor instrument (CFII) rating, which qualified me to teach other pilots to fly in the clouds. With my new flight instructor ratings I was able to obtain work at a local flight school near my home.

When I was first hired as a flight instructor it was initially an overwhelming experience. After all, I had acquired less than 400 total flight hours when I began instructing. However, what I learned then still resonates now. To teach any topic the instructor only has to know more than the students he or she is teaching. By the way, it is easy to be hired as a flight instructor as it seems flight schools are always looking to fill instructor positions because the instructors are always looking for better paying flying jobs.

In my opinion, the best way to improve your flying skills is to fly with a variety of student pilots and licensed pilots. You will learn something from every student with whom you fly. You will hopefully learn patience. If you don't acquire patience you will not be an effective instructor. An instructor must always remember that each student learns differently, and at learns their own pace. Like I said, if flying airplanes was easy everybody could become a pilot. It is not easy to become a pilot, that's why there is a shortage in the airline industry. If you choose to become a flight instructor, which I recommend, your student pilots will depend on your professionalism and talent to keep them safe.

The job of a flight instructor is not to be taken lightly. I found flight instructing to be difficult, but rewarding work. I won't spend more time on this topic because if you're reading this book your goal is probably to become an airline pilot, not a flight instructor. However, I will add that if you choose to earn your flight instructor rating, en-route to your airline career, and if you later find that you don't enjoy all the travel required of an airline pilot, you can always return to flight instructing. If you decide to resume employment as an instructor after having been an airline pilot, you will likely be the most "in demand" instructor in your flight school, and you can charge a higher hourly rate for your time. Or, you can instruct on your own, without having to work for a flight school. Why? Because most flight schools employ low-time instructor pilots who only plan on working at a flight school long enough to make the jump to an airline career. If you already have airline pilot credentials and you return to instructing, you will be the "big dog" in your flight school. Word will spread and most students in the school will want to train with the instructor who has already accomplished what they're striving for, an airline career!

If you fly an average of 20 hours weekly you will accumulate 1,040 flight hours in one year. You can fly more, or you can fly less. I suggest you fly as much as possible, because the quicker you're hired by a regional airline, the faster you'll be hired by a mainline carrier, and the sooner your paycheck will increase.

Airline Transport Pilot (ATP) Certificate

When you have accumulated at least 1,000 total flight hours it is time to begin studying for your airline transport pilot (ATP) written exam. To prepare for the written exam I purchased the Sheppard Air (www.sheppardair.com) ATP multi-engine online course for $75. I loaded the test preparation software on my iPad and studied up to three hours daily, for approximately two months. By the way, the requirements to earn your ATP certificate can be found in FAR 61.151.

I initially struggled to learn many of the concepts and information required to pass the ATP written exam. However, the online course allowed me to identify subject matter I did not understand. I then focused on that specific material until I had it mastered. When I felt I was prepared to take the written exam, I located an authorized testing facility. The exam is conducted on a secure computer and the testing room is monitored by either a person or a video camera. When I finally took the exam I received a passing score of 98%. A score of 70% is all that is required to pass the exam. However, I suspect that a passing score of only 70% on your ATP written test might be viewed negatively during an airline interview. Don't be good enough, be great!

Since July 31, 2014, the government has made it more difficult and expensive to obtain an ATP license (FAR 61. 156). The change was enacted after a regional airliner crashed in icing conditions, en-route to Buffalo, New York. The change in FAA regulations now requires an ATP pilot applicant to obtain a graduation certificate from an authorized facility, which requires 30 hours of classroom instruction and 10 hours of training in a flight simulation device. Fortunately, I had passed my ATP written exam before the change took effect. The increased training requirement has made it more expensive to obtain your ATP certificate. Forgive the bad news, but this is information you should know. However, the good news is this: Due to the pilot shortage, perhaps this added requirement will be rescinded, or at least modified so that the burden on pilots is less onerous and expensive. Otherwise, just continue on your path to the airline and only worry about this requirement when the time comes.

YOUR FIRST PILOT JOB

"If you have flown, perhaps you can understand the love a pilot develops for flight. It is much the same emotion a man feels for a woman or a wife for her husband."

Louise Thaden

After you obtain your single or multi-engine commercial pilot certificate, you are able to obtain paid employment as a pilot. As I mentioned earlier, most pilots elect to become flight instructors so that they are able to earn an income while accruing valuable flight time. However, if you choose not to pursue flight instructing, there are a few other options available. You might find a wealthy individual who is interested in hiring a low-time, inexperienced pilot. These jobs do exist, but they are similar to unicorns. You hear about these pilot jobs, but you haven't actually met a low-time pilot flying a wealthy business person to exotic locations. When I become a wealthy business person the last person I want at the controls of my airplane is a low-time pilot. There is no substitute for experience.

Fortunately, there are some jobs available to low-time pilots. Pilots might find employment towing gliders, banner towing, pipeline patrol, or even observing traffic for the local news. These jobs exist, as I have actually met pilots who accrued flight hours in these areas. Once a pilot has accrued in excess of 800 flight hours, more job opportunities may become available, such as package delivery, or even flying passengers in a Pilatus.

My suggestion is this; if you don't want to become a flight instructor, do not pursue that path. You won't enjoy the work. Pursue another flying job in order to continue accruing flight hours. If you're persistent, you will find a flying job. As more pilots move up the food chain to the airlines and corporate flying gigs, the more openings you will find for entry-level pilots. Like I said before, it is a good time to be a pilot.

APPLYING TO A REGIONAL AIRLINE

"The modern airplane creates a new geographical dimension. A navigable ocean of air blankets the whole surface of the globe. There are no distant places any longer: the world is small and the world is one."

Wendell Willkie

When you have completed the ATP written exam and have accumulated over 1,000 flight hours, submit an online application to the airline of your choice. Some things to consider when applying for a regional airline might be where their domiciles (bases) are located. If you live in California and want to be based in Los Angeles, you will want to apply to an airline with a base in Los Angeles. If you live on the West Coast, and are hired at an airline that only has domiciles on the East Coast, you will have to commute to work, or move to the East Coast. At this time, the airlines are competing for you, so apply to the airline that will best meet your needs.

Regional airlines often partner with the larger, domestic carriers, to serve smaller airports that are not economically viable to be served using larger aircraft. Regional airlines often fly Canadair Regional Jets (CRJ) and/or Embraer Regional Jets (ERJ).These jets carry between 50 and 76 passengers. These planes fly just as high and fast as any other jet, with some exceptions. Some regional airlines still fly turboprop aircraft. However, in my opinion, skip the turboprop and go right to the jet. There are a variety of regional airlines across the country. Some offer "flow through" to a major carrier and some pay better than others. I will not endorse a particular regional airline. By the time you have accrued over 1,000 flight hours you will have an idea where you want to work. Also, due to the ever increasing competition to recruit new pilots, regional carriers are currently offering generous signing bonuses and higher first-year pay, because they are competing for you!

I have heard horror stories about the working conditions at some airlines. However, airline pilots are notorious for their ability to complain. Many pilots have never had a job unrelated to flying and are unaware of the actual horror of sitting in a cubicle 40 hours weekly, so take their complaints with a grain of salt.

Each regional airline has their minimum requirements posted on their websites. For example, an internet search of one regional airline discovered the following minimums:

- 1,500 flight hours
- At least 21 years old
- 200 hours cross-country
- 100 hours night flight
- 75 hours instrument flight
- 25 hours actual multi-engine
- ATP written

These requirements change over time, so my suggestion is to simply get started, because accumulating flight hours takes time. As you accrue more flight hours, visit a regional airline website and investigate their minimum requirements. As the pilot shortage worsens it is possible that the FAA may have to relax the required minimums in order to sustain the flying needs of the country.

WHAT TO EXPECT AT A REGIONAL AIRLINE

"Ours is the commencement of a flying age, and I am happy to have popped into existence at a period so interesting."

Amelia Earhart

After you are hired by a regional airline you will attend ground school at the company's training facility, which might be located out-of-state from where you are currently living. The airline will pay you a basic salary while you are in training and will arrange for you to stay in a hotel. You might initially be assigned a roommate. My training class was comprised of approximately 40 new hire pilots. Nearly all the pilots had been employed as flight instructors before they were hired by my airline. Three pilots had been flying for the military, and one pilot had been employed as a crop duster. I had not been working as a pilot prior to being hired. Instead, I had been pushing papers for the government. I had allowed myself to be held captive behind a desk, staring at the clock, willing the workday to end. I had only been flying occasionally for fun, on the weekends. As such, I found airline ground school to be very challenging.

During the first day of training all new hire pilots attended orientation and completed a variety of routine paperwork, enrolled in the company health insurance plan, and signed up for various retirement benefits. We introduced ourselves to one another; submitted urine samples for drug screening; and were measured for uniforms.

On day two, we began learning about company policy and a host of other information.

On day three, we began learning aircraft systems, in detail, and at a fast pace.

During ground school I attended class for at least 8 hours daily. After class, the pilots studied in a small group setting. I found that I had to study 16 hours daily, either in class, or in a study group, just to keep my head above water. I did not return home on weekends, like some of my classmates. I was too busy studying.

All of the new pilots had to pass a variety of exams during training. If we failed to pass any exams we would have been dismissed from employment. Not all of the pilots in my training class were able to pass the required exams. The training was very demanding. Trying to understand and remember all the new information was similar to drinking water from a fire hose. It was too much knowledge to absorb, coming too fast. However, to prevent myself from falling behind, in addition to joining a study group, I also attended tutoring sessions, offered by the company pilot instructors during lunch breaks, and after class had ended. I was not alone in my struggle to master the information. After a quick meal, I studied until I my eyelids became too heavy. This routine lasted approximately three weeks. After much stress and frustration I successfully completed ground school, and then it was on to the flight training devices.

During the actual flight instruction portion of training, the newly hired pilots began studying "flows." A flow is a repetitive motion that pilots must learn, as flows are required during various phases of flight. For example, prior to beginning the first flight of the day, pilots verify flight deck switch positions in a specific sequence. This is known as a flow. The flows differ, depending on the phase of flight, and must be committed to memory.

After learning flows, we began training in basic flight simulator training devices to continue familiarizing ourselves with the location of various levers, knobs, and switches, etc. We also began learning how to program the flight computer and eventually we began combining the various aspects of training, so that we are able to simulate an actual flight.

Once the new hire pilots had demonstrated proficiency in basic flight training devices, my classmates and I began training in flight simulators. Flight simulators are impressive and very expensive representations of the aircraft flight deck. The simulators are suspended in air by several enormous pistons, which allow a realistic range of motion. The massive flight simulators are fitted with interior screens which replicate the aircraft windscreen. Images are presented on the screen, suggesting that the pilots are sitting in the actual plane, at a real airport, or are in flight. Also, every type of weather scenario can be presented on the screen. The instructor sits behind the pilots and manipulates the controls to provide a broad range of experiences, which might include system failures, deteriorating weather, wind shear, conflicting traffic, smoke in the cabin, and an endless selection of situations that airline pilots might, or will eventually encounter in the real world.

During training, you can expect to be assigned a flying partner. You will generally begin each training session by attending a two-hour classroom briefing, before each simulator event. The first officer may be the pilot flying (PF) for two hours, while the captain is assigned the role of pilot monitoring (PM). After two hours in the simulator, the pilots enjoy a 10-minute break, and then reverse roles.

You may find that your training session begins at 0200 hours and continues until 0800 hours in the morning. The simulator training could continue for four or five days before you receive a day to yourself.

Each phase of training requires the pilots to demonstrate proficiency before continuing on to the next phase of training.

I found the simulator training to be difficult and stressful. I had never flown a jet airplane prior to being hired by an airline and most of the flight time I had acquired had been in older, single-engine aircraft, usually equipped with primitive avionics and basic navigation systems. Also, the aircraft I had flown, before being hired by an airline, were generally fitted with only a few switches and knobs. Large commercial jet aircraft are seemingly equipped with hundreds of knobs, switches, dials, buttons, levers, and circuit breakers.

Flight simulator training may continue for two or three weeks. Part of your training will include taking the "practical" test for the airline transport pilot certificate (ATP). After passing the practical portion of your ATP certificate, you have earned the equivalent of a master's degree, in my opinion. You can sign "ATP" after your name, just like an MBA.

Earning an airline transport pilot certificate indicates that you are truly a professional pilot. You have reached the summit. You have trained and studied for hundreds or thousands of hours and demonstrated the ability to master a variety of subjects, such as meteorology; aerodynamics, mathematics, physics, electrical and hydraulic systems, physiology, and a host of other subject matter. It is quite an accomplishment and you will feel a sense of well-deserved pride for what you have achieved. This is the level of competence that the flying public warrants. After all, your friends and family deserve to have the best-trained aviators in the flight deck. But I caution you, the pressure really increases once you begin flying the actual airplane.

After you have completed simulator training and earned your ATP certificate, you can expect to complete additional training in the actual jet airplane, with paying passengers onboard. You will begin flying with a company check airman. A check airman is a captain who has been qualified to teach and evaluate other airline pilots. Check airmen have demonstrated a level of competency well above the average pilot, and they are able to fly the aircraft by themselves, if needed. As a new hire, you must demonstrate that you are competent and safe before the check airman will authorize you to begin flying with a "regular" captain.

You may be required to fly approximately 50 hours with the check airman before you qualify to "fly the line." When you report for your first day on the job, flying the actual jet aircraft, if you are like most of us you will feel totally overwhelmed. Not only will you probably be reporting for duty at an airport unknown to you, you will be unfamiliar with the door codes required to access the aircraft. You will be unsure where to place your luggage. You will be unfamiliar with the roles of the various ground crews. You will even be unsure how to operate the onboard radio. You will be a fish out of water. Believe me.

To help alleviate some of the overwhelming stress you might encounter on your first day of flying the actual airplane, prepare as much as possible in advance. Review the airport and taxiway diagrams. Study the possible departure procedures. Write down the door codes for the airports you will be visiting that day. Record the names of your fellow crew members. Make a note of the flight number for each leg of the day's route. Have access to as much information as possible because once you get settled into the right seat, things will move quickly. Remember to work at a pace that is comfortable to you and accept that you have much to learn. Most importantly, don't be too hard on yourself. It can take several months to feel comfortable as a new airline pilot. Just know that things will get better in time.

When you are first hired you will not have any seniority, so you will be based wherever the airline needs you. You can relocate to your domicile, or commute there. If commuting, you can travel free on most airlines, but you will fly "standby." Standby travel means you are not guaranteed to get a seat. However, when I commuted to Chicago, from Los Angeles, I almost always got a seat, even if I had to sit in the flight deck. Standby travel is also known as "non-revving. "Meaning, the airline is not earning any revenue from you as a passenger, so you are a low-priority passenger and will only get on the aircraft if an empty seat is available.

Many pilots who are based at LAX cannot afford to live in Los Angeles, so they buy homes in Phoenix, Arizona, and commute to work in Los Angeles. Commuting is no fun and can be stressful, but thousands of pilots commute because they choose to live outside their domicile. Fortunately, I was able to become domiciled at LAX within six months of being hired, so I can drive to the airport to begin a trip. Life is better when you don't have to commute!

As a new pilot, you will initially be placed on a "reserve" schedule. This means that you will be assigned a block of work days. While on reserve duty you are usually scheduled to work four days in a row, and you will be "on call" during those days. Meaning, you must report to the airport and be available to fly within two hours, if called. If you live in Phoenix and are based in Chicago, you will have to find accommodations in Chicago while you are on reserve, as you need to be able to get to O'Hare airport within two hours when you are on short-call reserve.

I paid for a "crash pad" in Chicago while I was based there and assigned to work a reserve schedule. A crash pad is a privately owned home, usually filled with bunk beds, often in a dormitory type setting. Some bunk beds are located in a bedroom, so a bedroom might only have two bunk beds, with a total of four mattresses in the room. Where I lived in Chicago the basement also contained 10 bunk beds. If your bunk is in the basement, you might hear other pilots snoring when you're trying to fall asleep. For that reason, I chose to pay a little more and I had a private bunk in a small bedroom, not in a dormitory setting.

Living in a crash pad sounds crazy, but it's not too bad. For one thing, pilots are usually flying when they are assigned to reserve duty, so there are only one or two pilots hanging around the crash pad at any given time. Also, it can be fun meeting other pilots from a variety of airlines. You will learn about the airline business, make new friends, and discover which airlines are hiring and where the best places are to work, etc.

I enjoyed my time in Chicago. I explored the city and had a great time. I paid $375 monthly for a bottom bunk. During my time there I never had to share my room, as the other pilots who had bunks in my room were never at the crash pad when I was there. You can find crash pads by searching the Internet. Almost any city with an airport served by an airline will have crash pads available for rent. You can choose to stay in a "pilot only" crash pad, or a "male-only" crash pad, or even a co-ed crash pad if you desire. I stayed in a "pilot only" crash pad while based in Chicago.

Following my stay in Chicago, I was based in a different city, closer to home. I advertised myself on Craigslist and found a private room in my new domicile for only $250 monthly. I was assigned to fly out of the second domicile for only a few months before LAX was assigned as my domicile. I was assigned LAX because I had requested to be based there. Now that I am based in Los Angeles I don't need a crash pad, but I rent a studio apartment close to the airport so that I can purposely bid a reserve schedule. A reserve schedule allows me lots of free time, as I am rarely called to fly while on reserve duty, because I have more seniority than most other pilots on reserve. Most pilots prefer to avoid reserve duty, as they want to fly as much as possible, and don't want to have to pay for a crash pad. While I am on reserve, if I am not called to fly, I am able to write books, like this one, in addition to my first book, *A BETTER LIFE* and my most recent book, *Happy Wife – Happy Life; A Survival Guide*. (Update: I have since changed my schedule and now work a fixed schedule. I work 12 days monthly and that is enough for me. Many pilots prefer to work 20 days monthly or more)

Once you qualify to bid for a "non-reserve" schedule, you can request to work a variety of schedules. Some pilots prefer to work 4-day trips, others prefer 3-day trips. Some pilots prefer to work "locals," which mean they fly during the day and return home in the afternoon. Other pilots prefer "stand-ups." Stand-up trips require pilots to fly one leg in the evening, stay overnight at their destination, and then fly home early in the morning. For example, a pilot might choose to fly the last flight of the night from LAX to Phoenix. The crew will sleep a few hours in Phoenix, and then fly the first flight of the day from Phoenix, back to LAX, and they are done. The pilots can earn several hours of pay for a short trip like this and still have the entire day to themselves. Many pilots with seniority bid these flights so they can be home during the day to be with their family.

Pilots can also "pick up" and "post" trips assigned to them. If a pilot posts a trip, another pilot might pick up their trip to earn extra money. Flying schedules can be very flexible. The higher you rise on the seniority list the better your schedule will become.

When a flight crew has a multi-day trip scheduled, the flight might depart early in the morning, and the day's flights may be completed by noon. If you're done flying at noon, you will have time to explore the city where you'll be staying overnight. Or you can relax. It's up to you. Sometimes, you might begin flying later in the day and fly late into the evening. Occasionally, I will fly just one leg (point A to point B) and have the remainder of the day to explore the city where I am staying overnight. Or, sometimes I finish my trip late in the evening and only have time to eat in my room, get some sleep, and wake early to depart the following day.

My airline has agreements with a variety of hotels throughout North America and generally we have very pleasant accommodations. When the flight crew arrives at our final destination, the hotel sends a shuttle van to pick up the crew at the airport. Each crew member generally tips the driver $1 for the ride to the hotel. We tip the driver another dollar on the return trip to the airport. I think this is absurd given that airplane passengers never tip me for flying the airplane, nor should they. I am just doing my job. My airline has an agreement with each hotel where we stay which requires a microwave and fridge either be in our room, or made available to us somewhere in the hotel.

I carry lots of food with me when I leave on a trip as I tend to eat healthier and save money using this strategy. The airline pays a "per diem" dollar amount for each overnight stay. I save that (tax-free) money and invest it. Other pilots spend lots of money eating at the airport and hotel restaurants. However, I make it a point to never purchase food at the airport and I only eat out occasionally when traveling. I figure I can save $30 dollars or more daily, just by avoiding expensive airport and hotel food.

My usual schedule requires me to work 4 days on duty, with 2-4 days off in between. I like to have Friday and Saturday off work so I can spend some time with my wife. Usually, each month, I will have four consecutive days off from flying. When I get four days off, I like to travel to Hawaii for a couple of nights. I fly free and always find inexpensive lodging so my wife can't complain. This is one of the benefits of becoming an airline pilot. An airline pilot can literally walk up to the counter at almost any airline and ask to get on a flight if there is an open seat. Sometimes, I have to book the travel online, or call the airline directly to get on a flight, but it is usually not too difficult to just get on the plane and go. (Update: I now prefer to work the first 2 weeks of the month and take off the remainder of the month)

When I was first hired by my airline in 2015, I earned $24 for each flight hour. While still in ground school, my pay increased to $30 per flight hour. After two years, I am earning $43 per flight hour. I just learned yesterday that another pay raise is coming soon. It's a good time to be an airline pilot. Mind you, the pay clock starts when the cabin door is closed, so there is a lot of time when I am not being paid. For example, I might have a 3-hour break in San Francisco, in the middle of my work day, and I am not getting paid for that time. The airline pays pilots by "block/credit time." If I only fly for a total of 4 hours in a day, I may get paid for 6 hours of block time. It may have taken me 9 hours or more to earn 6 hours of pay. The airline pay system is confusing and I can't say I totally understand it. Actually, I don't understand it. I can say, however, that nearly all pilots complain about their pay. If a pilot is earning $24 hourly, or $240 hourly, they complain that they're underpaid. I am speaking from experience. I have sat in the jump seat while flying to Hawaii many times and the pilots earning over $200 hourly are still complaining about their pay. I think it is a job requirement to complain about the pay, but these pilots keep showing up and most say there is no other job they would want.

My company also offers health care and a 401k retirement plan with a "match." The match means my company will contribute up to 6% of the money I allocate toward my retirement account. I consider the employer match to be "free money," so I always contribute at least up to the match amount. The health care plan is basic and I suspect it is about as good as you might find in most other professions; meaning it could be better.

The upgrade time to captain varies at each regional airline, but I have heard stories of first officers upgrading to captain within six months at other airlines. That's scary, in my opinion. It takes time to gain the experience required of an airline captain. At my airline, for example, the current time to upgrade to captain is approximately two years. The upgrade time also varies based on the needs of the airline. If the pilot shortage continues, as I expect it will, upgrade times will continue to come down.

When I report to work I show up about an hour prior to my flight and I print a flight release, conduct an inspection of the aircraft, and get settled into the flight deck. The captain is in charge of the flight, but the captains I fly with are not my bosses. I answer to the Chief Pilot at my domicile. I have never actually met my Chief Pilot. The captain and first officer work as a team, in conjunction with the flight attendants, to ensure a safe and on-time departure and arrival. We all understand what is expected and we complete our duties as trained. There is nobody breathing down our necks like you might find in most workplaces. This is another great thing about being an airline pilot. You are working with other professionals. It takes hard work, dedication, and intelligence to become an airline pilot, unlike some other places where I have worked, namely the government. That's another book, for another day.

LEARN THIS AND YOUR JOURNEY WILL BE EASIER, FASTER, AND LESS EXPENSIVE

"Aeronautics was neither an industry nor a science. It was a miracle."

Igor Sikorsky

You may find that learning to fly can be frustrating because flying an airplane is dissimilar from driving a car. It takes time and persistence to become proficient at flying. You will experience sensory overload and you might feel overwhelmed on occasion. If you're like most people, you can drive your car, engage in a conversation, change lanes, tune your stereo, read highway signs, and eat a sandwich while you are cruising down the highway at 65 mph. However, when you first began driving, it took all your concentration just to complete a turn without hitting the curb. You learned to drive without the radio playing and usually without too many other cars nearby. It took time for driving to become second nature. If you learned to drive a car equipped with a stick shift, it probably took all your concentration just to shift from 1st to 2nd gear. However, in time you were able to shift without even thinking. Learning to fly is no different. It takes time and repetition to become a good pilot. Don't be too hard on yourself when you begin training. You will figure it out.

When you're learning to fly general aviation aircraft, you will immediately discover that on the ground, you steer the aircraft using your feet. Unlike a car, where you don't have to talk with "car traffic control," in an airplane, you have to communicate with air traffic control (ATC). You must be aware of nearby aircraft during taxi. You have to navigate on the airport tarmac via a specific set of instructions. You must interpret and comply with various signs located on the taxiway and runways. Your flight instructor will often talk to you while you're trying to listen to ATC and figure out where you're at on the ground. There can be a lot going on before you ever get in the air. It's too much for your brain to interpret early on and you might feel stressed out. This is normal. Know that maneuvering an airplane on the ground and in flight will eventually become second nature. To alleviate some stress when you're learning to fly, listen to ATC on your computer or phone in your free time. You will discover that air traffic control and pilots repeat the similar information, over and over and over. "Pilot speak" is similar to learning a new language. Once I discovered that the same information is continually being requested and provided, the task of learning the new pilot language became less daunting.

Pilots make contact with ATC by stating who they are, where they are, and what they want. ATC will usually respond with your call sign and tell you where to go, how to get there, and what to expect. For example, early in your training, at an airport populated with general aviation aircraft and a control tower, you can expect to make contact with ATC and you might say on the radio, "Fullerton tower. Cessna 123. 10 miles west at 3,000', request landing with information Yankee." ATC may respond, "Cessna 123. Continue eastbound, expect right traffic runway 24, and call abeam the tower." The term "Yankee" relates to the current conditions at the airport, also known as the ATIS. Before arriving at an airport, a pilot must listen to the automated terminal information system (ATIS). Each hour the ATIS is updated and a new phonetic identifier is assigned, such as alpha, bravo, charlie, etc. You must provide the appropriate phonetic identifier when you contact your intended airport of arrival, or provide the phonetic identifier to approach control if you're in contact with them.

The sooner you learn "pilot speak," the easier learning flying becomes because it is one less thing you have to think about. It won't take too long to feel comfortable communicating in "pilot speak." Brief and concise communication with ATC is expected and appreciated on the radio. Using YouTube, you can search, "Talking to ATC" and find lots of helpful videos which will provide great examples of what you can expect when communicating with air traffic control.

You will also reduce your frustration if you quickly learn what the markings and signs on the tarmac, taxiways, and runways signify. You will be required to know this information eventually, so learn it sooner rather than later. Again, search YouTube by typing, "Airport signs and markings." By watching aviation videos you will advance much faster in your training. In fact, you can benefit from the thousands of YouTube videos created by other pilots, which explain nearly every topic related to flying. If you're having trouble with a particular concept while studying at home, search for the flight maneuver or exam questions online. Watching online training videos may help you "get the big picture" and your flight training will be less frustrating and even less expensive. I freely admit that I reviewed many YouTube videos when I was preparing for my airline interview, and several videos were very helpful.

CONCLUSION

"We want the air to unite the peoples, and not to divide them."

Lord Swinton

Like I said at the beginning of the book, the only obstacle preventing you from becoming an airline pilot is you. You are capable of succeeding at anything I have mentioned in this book.

I also want to mention what you might expect during your interview with an airline. First, you should know that there are "gouges" available online. The gouges detail the scenarios you might encounter and the questions you may be asked during your interview. You can prepare for the interview by studying the various online gouges. Just enter "airline interview gouge" in your web browser and you will find a variety of gouges. Some pilots pay hundreds of dollars to attend seminars, where they learn the same material discussed in the online gouges. Save your money. I did not attend, nor did I pay to attend any seminar which promised to help me get hired. Instead, I read the online gouges and prepared accordingly.

Here is what I did to get hired by a regional airline. Like I mentioned, I studied several gouges until I felt confident that I could respond appropriately to any possible question or scenario. Then, during the actual interview, I presented my authentic-self. I arrived early; I was wearing a sports coat, tie, slacks, and dress shoes. My hair was cut appropriately and I was clean shaven. I was polite, professional and humble, but confident.

Two active airline captains conducted the interview. I told each captain that I was grateful and appreciative to have been given the opportunity to interview, which was true. When they asked about me, I was honest and forthcoming, and I also asked about them. They asked my interests and I asked about theirs.

If you are interviewed by airline captains, not someone from Human Resources, I suspect that the actual captains will really want to learn one thing. That is, "Would I want to sit a few feet away from this person, for four days, often in stressful situations?" If the interviewers can't see themselves sharing their workspace with you, your chances of being hired may be in jeopardy.

The captains and first officers work as a team, and the ability to get along with each other makes for a great trip. Flying with a person who is negative, bitter, grouchy, and hostile is a terrible experience. Be the pilot that everybody enjoys flying with. If that's you, just be yourself during the interview. If that's not you, solicit advice on how you might improve your people skills.

Thank you for reading my second book. If you enjoyed my writing, please tell a friend and take a minute and leave a positive 5-star review on Amazon or wherever you purchased the book. Also, consider purchasing my other books, such as, **A Day In The Life Of An Airline Pilot.** Or my latest book, **Happy Wife – Happy Life, A Survival Guide.** You will also enjoy my first book, **A BETTER LIFE: Goal Setting, Visualization, & The Law Of Attraction.** I appreciate your support as I fulfill my dream of becoming a successful author and speaker, just as I was able to fulfill my dream of becoming an airline pilot!

Happy flying!

Warm regards,
Robert Lawrence, ATP

AVIATION TERMS & DEFINITIONS

"Man must rise above the Earth — to the top of the atmosphere and beyond — for only thus will he fully understand the world in which he lives."

Socrates

AIM: Aeronautical Information Manual. The Federal Aviation Administration publishes the AIM and it is available online. The AIM contains a variety of information useful to pilots.

CFI: Certified Flight Instructor

CFII: Certified Flight Instructor/Instrument. A CFII may provide flight instruction toward an instrument rating.

Class rating: A class rating is a classification of aircraft, within a particular category. Aircraft classes include singe engine and multi-engine, etc.

Commercial pilot: A commercial pilot certificate allows a pilot to earn income from flying. A pilot with only a private pilot license is generally prohibited from earning income as a pilot.

FAA: Federal Aviation Administration

FBO: Fixed Base Operator. An FBO is a business located at an airport. An FBO may sell fuel; provide flight instruction, and offer aircraft parking, etc.

Flight certificate: A pilot's license, also known as a pilot "certificate," authorizes a pilot to fly a specific "category" of aircraft, such as: "Airplane." There is a total of seven separate aircraft categories, to include rotorcraft, and glider, etc. The most common aircraft certificate earned is, "private pilot – single engine land."

Flight rating: A flight rating is "added on" to a pilot certificate and indicates that a pilot has mastered a particular type of flying, such as instrument flying, or flying a multi-engine aircraft.

IFR: Instrument Flight Rules. This means you are complying with rules outlined FAA Part 91. 167. IFR rules have different requirements for fuel, weather conditions, and required aircraft equipment, etc.

IMC: Instrument Meteorological Conditions. This generally means that you are flying in the clouds or in reduced visibility weather conditions.

Instrument rating: An instrument rating basically means the pilot is authorized to fly in the clouds, subject to IFR regulations, via an instrument flight plan, under a variety of conditions.

MEI: Multi-engine Instructor. An MEI is authorized to provide flight instruction in multi-engine aircraft.

Practical exam: The practical exam is the actual flying portion of your flight test, as opposed to the written portion of a flight test.

VMC: Visual Meteorological Conditions. This generally means you are flying in good visibility conditions.

VFR: Visual Flight Rules. VFR rules apply to flights operating is skies with good visibility.

ABOUT THE AUTHOR

ROBERT LAWRENCE is an airline pilot, sailor, adventurer, and an author of two books. He served in the US Army 3/75th Ranger Regiment from 1985-86 and is a graduate of the University of Washington in Seattle. He currently lives in Southern California with his wife and two rescue cats.

Also by Robert Lawrence;

- **A BETTER LIFE; Goal Setting, Visualization, & the Law of Attraction**
- **A Day In The Life Of An Airline Pilot**
- **Happy Wife – Happy Life; A Survival Guide**

47605201R00045

Made in the USA
Columbia, SC
02 January 2019